When it rains...

Robert Gutzmer

Edited by: Matt Miller

authorHOUSE®

AuthorHouse™
1663 Liberty Drive
Bloomington, IN 47403
www.authorhouse.com
Phone: 1-800-839-8640

First published by AuthorHouse 8/25/2011

ISBN: 978-1-4634-4271-2 (e)
ISBN: 978-1-4634-4272-9 (sc)

Library of Congress Control Number: 2011914112

Printed in the United States of America

Dedicated to: My friends and Family
for keeping me going

"People often write about what they don't understand"

Table of Contents

LOVE

DEATH

LIFE

LOVE

"Wounds on the heart never heal,
they just stop bleeding.
Scars never go away."

Only When I Think Of Her
02/26/2003

Only when I think of her
Do I have a smile on my face
Only when I think of her
Is it not so dark in this place
Only when I think of her
Do my Problems drift away
Only when I think of her
Am I grateful for every day
Only when I think of her
Does my heart skip a beat
Only when I think of her
Can I accomplish any feat
Only when I think of her
Do I pick up the phone
Only when I think of her
Do I cry cause I'm alone

Sleep
05/11/2003

A man lies awake, in the middle of the night
Thinking to himself, about what's wrong and
what's right
Thinking about old times, and what's to come
Thinking about yesterday's her, and all the fun
It hurts to think of her, when he knows there's
someone new
He thinks about the happiness, and starts to
feel blue
A new love forbidden, like Romeo and Juliet
Old love on his mind, he can't ever forget

I lie awake at night, the pressure never stops
My eye lids get heavy and fill with tear drops
My future looking dim, there's pain ahead
Pain in other hearts, because of what I said

I lie awake at night, tired from the day
Tomorrow when I look at them, what will I
say?

The holes I've dug, for me are getting deep
The pressure never stops... until I fall asleep

4

Rainy Day
03/12/2003

Dressed in all black
      I sit outside
      They said it wouldn't rain
      But they lied

Dressed in all black
      My hood on my face
      Trying to get away
      I just need my space

Dressed in all black
      A tear in the rain
      The growing of sorrow
      The growing of pain

Dressed in all black
      Head down at the floor
      Feeling so empty
      I can't take it anymore

      Consumed by the thought
      What in my soul do I lack
      I sit here thinking
Dressed in all black

You Give Me Strength
07/03/2003

My friends
>   They give me strength too

My family
>   They give me strength too

My thoughts
>   They give me strength too

My heart
>   It gives me strength too

But my love
>   Is given just to you

Days
07/05/2003

One of these days
 Doubt will leave your mind
 And the words you say
 Will be more then just kind
 And the things we do
 Will be for us
 We will make love
 Out of trust

 I'll make love to
 Your body and mind
 And the hole in my heart
 Will be filled with the love we find
 We'll both be happy
 As we sit in praise
 Just me and you
One of these days

Future
07/25/2003

I dream of my kids
And you're there too
I dream of my house
And you're there too
I dream of my family
And you're there too
I dream of my friends
And you're there too
Now tell me what my life would be like
*   If I didn't have you*

True Love
07/28/2003

When you love something
       With all of your might
And you try so hard to get it
       With every breath you fight
But you get no where
       And it doesn't seem to be
You tend to give up
       In hopes they will see
Your heart is broke
       And you feel so drained
Your heart has a spot
       A permanent stain
An empty hole where
       Love once stood
I won't love anyone else
       Not even if I could

Never Felt Before
09/10/2003

The days seem to grow longer, the nights too
Nothing left for me here, this I know is true
The only thing I have left is anger, building inside
All the blood I've shed, all the tears I've cried

Many a days I've wished that this would all end
All the things I wanted to say in the letters I couldn't
send
Everything seems dark now, and it's harder to fight
I feel alone during the day, but feel it more at night

The scars I can't hide, the pain still grows
The devil may cry, but no one knows
Alone for now, alone till a new
Alone till the day, I finally find you

One Love
12/19/2003

As I sit here and think
I can't help but pray
That, "I love you"
Is what you'll one day say

I've tried everything
To get your love
You're not like the rest
You I put far above

Everything I've ever said
You can be sure it's true
There's no doubt in my mind
That I love you

I could make you happy
I could give you the stars
I could be your shoulder
I could heal your scars

I could be your shield
Together like glue
Rap my arms around
And let nothing hurt you

My Everything
12/26/2003

We belong together
But as I try to make it be
I can see you resisting
At the thought of you and me
I cry invisible tears
And weep over you
I've tried everything
What else can I do?
One sided love
Like a dagger to my chest
Our life together
My eternal quest
With one more chance
You could be my queen
But instead I cry
At the future I've seen
My tears fall to the page
As I walk the earth alone
Nothing is absolute
Everything is unknown

If
02/03/2005

I awake to your face
A picture in my mind
I thought in my dream
I left you behind
When I see you cry
My heart does break
Your face in my mind
Asleep or awake
When you're unhappy
I am too
And when you need someone to listen
I'm right next to you
You're my happiness
You're the sun in my sky
And without you in my life
I would surely want to die
But when I get to heaven
The angels would say
I did nothing but watch over you
Each and every day

The Perfect Love
10/25/2006

"They are so perfect together"
Their friends use to say
"She's always kissing him"
"And he's always holding her that way"
"Look at how they look at each other"
"And how they smile"
"And how they say good-bye with love"
"And how she cries when he's gone awhile"
They are like the perfect pair
A touch of true love
He was her angel
And she was his dove
Their fights lasted minutes
And their make up lasted hours
Two loves showing
The strength of loves power
It seemed that nothing
Would ever break them apart
It seemed that nothing
Could break these lovers hearts

It was just another trip
Just a few months long
The war was calling
And the call was strong
So he packed his things
And said he'd write
He promised to come back

After the fight
They promised their love
As she started to cry
He wiped her tear
And they said their good-byes

He wrote when he could
She wrote everyday
"I miss you and love you"
The same things they'd always say
He told his friends
"She's my gift you see"
She told her friends
"He's coming home to me"

Then one day
With a Knock at the door
She seen the uniform
And fell to the floor
"Ma'am I'm sorry,
To be the one to say
But he took on heavy fire
And he couldn't get away."
"All we found were his tags
And this picture of you."
Her life was in pieces
And he was the glue

She cried for days
Just holding his tags
At the funeral they presented
A folded up flag

Friends looked on
With little to say
She felt so empty
And it never went away
She never left the house
Out the window she gazed
Months went by
But it felt like days
Months turned to years
As family asked why
"Why do you sit here
And do nothing but cry?"

"They never found his body
So I'll sit by the phone
He's still out there
And he promised to come home."

Love
11/29/2006

I want love
The kind of love that makes you long for their return
The kind of love that makes your heart burn
The kind of love where a kiss is enough to make you warm
The kind of love beyond the norm
The love that makes you gently touch her skin
Where a closed eye kiss can make the room spin
You kiss her hand, and play with her hair
She kisses your chest, and doesn't mind if you stare
Because she knows she can't help but stare at you
And you know the same is true

I want love
The kind of love that grabs you and won't let go
The kind of love that can pick you up when you are low
The kind of love only spoken of
Yea… that's my kind of love
The love where you call them to say I love you
And as soon as they answer they say I love you too
The love that makes you stay always alert
Because you would rather die then see them hurt
You can make her bither lip and her body shake
She can make your toes curl and raise the stake

I want love
The movie romances, the perfect emotion
As high as the sky, and as deep as the ocean
That's the love I want....no need
And every day with god I plead
I don't know if it will come
Or who it will be from
But I know that just for me
It's only that love that will set me free
Because that love only comes with fate
So until then, I will sit....hope....and wait

Dark Night
01/08/2007

The night is dark
There is no sound
As I hold you
You hear my heart pound
I move my hand to your neck
And softly lift your head
Our eyes connect
Your lips are red
We kiss and touch
Your skin so smooth
Our lips never part
As together we move
My hands to your shirt
As it drops to the ground
Your hands to my pants
As they also come down
Our bodies touch
As if to be one
Our kisses so soft
But the story's not done
I move to your chest
As you start breathing fast
I kiss your stomach
But quickly move past
As I come to your thigh
My tongue starts to quiver
You whisper, "Don't stop"
As your body starts to shiver
As I taste you
You grab the bed
You close your eyes
And push on my head
You bite your lips

As you reach your max
Then your body goes numb
And your muscles relax
You pull me up
And roll me on top of you
But you have to pause
And wait for part two

Part Two
01/08/2007

We roll around
You end up on top
Though the position changes
The kissing doesn't stop
I grab at your hair
You scratch at my chest
Our wild passion
Isn't like the rest
My fingers find their way down
And your hand begins to play
"Maybe I should go....?"
"No .....please....stay!"
We torment each other
As the anticipation grows
It feels so good
You can feel it in your toes
As I enter
Your head lifts high
I move deep inside
"Harder" you cry
You start to ride
And move your hips
I start to thrust
And bit my lips
My hand on your waist
The sound of our embrace
Your moan gets louder
As the speed does increase
I grab you close
And roll to the side
Now I'm on top

And in control of this ride
A thrust of my body
As we get close......together
I'll shield you from the world
No matter the weather
I tease your lips
But you need that kiss
Cause the taste of each other
We both know we miss
You dig into my back
The climax grabs you
You breathe in my ear
This makes me finish too
Our bodies touching
Breathing faster
You body shaking
For minutes after
Your fingers go numb
As the room quiets down
You start to whisper
The softest sound

"Don't ever leave,
Stay close to me."

"Then I will hold you close
For eternity!"

What "It" Is
01/17/2007

The thought of me and you brings a smile to my face
"IT's" what keep us close despite the space
I love your smile and the things you do
You asked me what I was thinking but you already knew
The way I hold you or a soft little kiss
The scratches on my back, the times I miss
Cuddling in bed. You call me a nerd
A hicky on my neck, so you can mark what's yours
But "IT'S" not just that, "IT'S" that look in your eyes
"IT'S" that feeling I know you have, deep down inside
"IT'S" the times you tell me to call as soon as I get up
But I know you're so tired that answering the phone is tough
"IT'S" when you know what I'm thinking and exactly when
I smile
And you know what to say to make me stay up a while
You don't have to tell me I'm special or tell me how I make
you feel
You don't have to tell me "IT'S" not fake because I know
"IT'S" real
Just tell me you're happy when you do what you do
And that you know "IT'S" worth it….. "IT'S" worth it to
you

I Don't Blame You
01/23/2007

I blame the sunset
    And the way it made you look
I blame the clock
    And all the time it took
I blame the drinks
    For making me strong
I blame the passion
    But it didn't feel wrong
I blame the sheets
    And the way they touched your skin
I blame my heart
    For letting you in
I blame myself
    Because this is true
    No matter what happens
I can't seem to blame you

Willing To Try
01/30/2007

I am not good with trust
Or the ability to rely
I am not good with faith
Or looking to the sky
I am not good with anger
Or holding it in
I am not good with regret
Because I like where I've been
I am not good with tears
Or letting my feelings show
I am not good with being open
And all this you know
But I am good with you
And THAT love is why

Because love to me....
Means you're willing to try

I Just Started Drinking
02/8/2007

Sitting by myself in this room all alone
Thinking about her....I call her on the phone
"Baby it's just me, I've had a couple beers....
My mind is going crazy, my eyes are dripping tears
Let me make you mine, let me and you be us
No more putting this off, right now it's a must."
She says I'm just drunk, and she doesn't know what to say
"Just tell me it's a yes and everything will be okay!"

She says, "It's been a long day, call me tomorrow
You just drank too much, we'll talk when you're sober."

"I want to talk now!" I'm beginning to shout
"The alcohol's just making the sober words come out."

She says, "My feeling are strong, I just don't know what to do."

"I'm sorry I can't help, the way I feel about you."

She says, "I need a little more time, please just understand."

"I can't just keep waiting, my heart is in your hand.
It hurts everyday, I know I'm not with you."
She's starting to tear up....what am I to do?
"Baby please forgive me, I think this is good-bye"

She says, "Did you call just to make me cry?"

"I'm sorry how this ends, I just don't understand
Is it really that hard to just call me your man?"

She says, "Please don't hang-up, what's going on in you head?"

"I can't stay on the phone, and say the same things I've said."
I grab another beer, after hanging up the phone
I sit....with my thoughts....I sit all alone

I See You Hurting
02/12/2007

I can see you are hurting
	And how you try and hide
I can see you are afraid
	But never have you lied
I can see you are tired
	And how you wanted to rest
I can see you are not sure
	For you what is the best

But I can see your smile
	When we talk on the phone
And I can see your sadness
	When you wish I were home
And I can see your love
	In the words that you do say
And I can see your feelings
	Each and everyday

But I can only hope
	That YOU can begin to see
All the love I have for you
	So together we can be

Butterfly
02/14/2007

The look in your eyes
   The flow of your hair
      The touch of your lips
         That's why I hold you near
The honest little thoughts
   The "I miss you" that you say
      The "I can't wait to see you"
         That's why I feel this way
The sweet things that you do
   The talks that last all night
      The smile you give me
         That's why I hold you tight
The curve of your body
   The silk of your skin
      The feel of your legs
         That's why I let you in
The often funny comments
   The faces that you make
      The caring that you give
         That's why my heart you take
You ask me why this happens
   And why my heart out pours
      It's in hopes that one day soon
         You will let my love take yours

Words
07/9/2007

Words fall short of their meaning
They just don't seem to fit
I try to describe how I feel
But the words are off a bit
I have a list of things....
This list of feelings I want to say
And when I try to tell you
The words just get in the way

If I combine words together
That would tell you how I feel
Make up my own words
Like Amazingly-Wonderful-Surreal
It would mean I daydream
Of touching your skin
Of holding your hand
And kissing your chin
I would make some words stronger
Armed with a paper and pen
Make some words magnified
Like desire or love times ten
It would mean unconditional
You I truly treasure
It would mean I promise
It would mean forever and ever
I would take some silly words
And add them to what I feel
Make my own language
Like comfy-fuzzy-sex-appeal
It would mean a warm hug
Mixed with a cute smile
It would mean your laugh
When I hold you awhile

My feelings just don't have words
That helps to show their real
So I came up with new ones
To show how I feel
And although these words won't catch on
And won't be used today
I-Love-You-So-Very-Much
It means in every way

29

Clock
06/17/2007

I wish I could hold you and wipe your tears away
I wish I could be there to tell you it's okay
Though this world holds us and keeps us apart
When I dream at night, I hold you in my heart
In the dream world, I softly kiss your head
I don't want to let you go. My sanctity is my bed
Miles apart I whisper to the skies and wish upon the
stars
I shout the words I love you, in hopes you'll hear my
calls
I pray to all the gods, to join together and fight
To turn the course of the heavens and make
everything alright
I ask the earth to spin real fast, and make the time
go by
So that my arms stay warm, with you close by my
side
Nothing ever changes. My wishes fall apart
My hopes seem to fade, but you stay in my heart

Just when I think
How will we get through
You tell me that you love me
And that your love is true
If the gods all get angry
Or if the stars do fall
If my arms grow cold
And the earth doesn't move at all
I know one thing is certain
I know one thing is true
I know I'll wait forever
Because I know that I love you too

Compared to my love
11/16/2007

I will take you to a beach and silhouetted against the
sand
I will point out into the darkness as I slowly grab your
hand
I will lay down a blanket...no...no...two blankets
So that we can roll around like the animals we want to
be
So that we can make love, together in an epic battle, just
you and me
And after I will rap the moon around us like a blanket
And place the stars next to us like night lights
And watch the glow from them take our passion to new
heights
As the ocean crushes the sand
And as the sun greets us in the morning
But even that, compared to my love, even that would be
boring

And I want to woo you
I want to take a rocket to the heavens and sit with you at
a table draped in a cloud
So that you can feel the rain, see the lighting spark and
hear the thunder get loud
After we will gaze on the earth like gods from a throne
And our worshipers will know of our passion through
my screams and your moans
And the sun will greet us in the morning
But even that, compared to my love, even that would be

boring

But I need to woo you
I have this need to take you to faraway lands and
romantic scenes
Where my words and actions bring the love in my heart
together with your dreams
Where every breath you take is free of worry fear and
doubt
Where my love remains paralyzed, because with you
gone I am with out
With out happiness, with out love, with out smiles and
with out action
I need to take you to a place inside my heart to show you
my love and growing attraction
Where the sun can greet us in the morning
But even that, compared to my love, even that would be
boring

But I will woo you
I will build for you a house with my two hands
Where our family and our future can stand
I will raise for you as many kids as you could care for
Give you the last of everything, and open every door
Now I am no knight, I have no armor and ride no
steed
But I will make sure you never hurt and never need
I will kiss you good-night and hold you until
The sun greets us in the morning
And that, for you that is just my love over pouring

DEATH

*"It's funny when you think about it,
the easiest death to handle
will be your own."*

THE TRUTH
04/27/2003

I WANT TO LOVE
I WANT TO DIE
I WANT TO FEEL
I WANT TO CRY
I HURT MYSELF
AND MAKE ME BLEED
I ASK FOR DEATH
AND WITH GOD I PLEAD
TOO MUCH ON MY MIND
AND YOU'RE NOT HERE
SO WHEN I DIE
DON'T SHED A TEAR
THIS IS TO ALL MY FRIENDS
YOU MEAN THE WORLD TO ME
BUT HOW DO I SAY...
WHAT WILL SET ME FREE?
MY HEART IS COLD
I FEEL EMPTY INSIDE
I SAID "LIFE GOES ON"
BUT I LIED

IT DOESN'T FOR ME
BECAUSE I'M ALL DONE
BEHIND THE CLOUDS
I FOUND NO SUN
FOR THE LAST TIME I SAY
I'VE HAD ENOUGH
I WANT TO DIE
LIFE'S TOO TOUGH

Empty
05/16/2003

Outside an empty house
On an empty street
There stands an empty man
Wet from head to feet

He sits there on his porch
Head down at the floor
No one is at home
Mom went to the store

The rain is getting heavy
Lighting in the sky
Loneliness in his heart
If only he knew why

He covers his face with a hood
Thoughts in his head
Newport in his hand
As he thinks of what she said

He loved her so much
But he had to let her go
The love wasn't shared

...or at least he thought so

Inside and empty house
On the same empty street
        She lies in her own blood
        Her maker she will meet

Ghost Rider
06/15/2003

In the dark and black of night
   On a walk near bark and wood
      A fog moves in so slow
         You can't see where you just stood
            You think the fog calls your name
               As your fear starts to rise
                  It can't be what you think
                     You slowly close your eyes
                     Alone in the woods with fear
                     Can cause your mind to snap
                  You hear the rider coming
               From the silent hoof tap
            You slowly turn your body
         As your face goes pale
      You open your eyes to find
   Nothing but an empty trail

Dying to be with you
07/05/2003

He rushes home...
She said she would call...
He can barely get his keys out...
As he runs down the hall...
She'll say she loves him...
So he sits waiting...
He questions her love...
In his mind he's debating...
An hour passes by...
And then two...
Maybe she doesn't care...
If only he knew...
Three hours have passed...
And still no call...
It's hard to pick yourself up...
After you fall...
Maybe it was a cruel joke...
She thinks she's so smart...
It hurts so bad...
This weak broken heart...
He cuts his wrist...
To die alone...
Meanwhile she laughs and jokes...

On her way home...
She starts to dial...
Not caring about a thing...
Meanwhile, the last thing he
hears...
. . .
Is the phone ring...

Death
08/11/2003

I fall asleep one day after hours of being awake:
         I see myself dead, "This must be a mistake!"
         I'm alone in a casket in the front of a hall
         Everyone sits around...my mom starts to ball
         I'm in a black suit, with one red rose
         My arms across my chest in a chilling pose
         My friends and family take turns getting up
         and talking
         Death points to the back of the room, so I
         start walking

         In the back of the hall far away from
         everyone
         Sits a woman who looks like she's carrying a
         ton
         Her face was still, she couldn't even cry
         She felt empty, and she knew exactly why
         "I didn't know she loved me this much!"
         She didn't know that was going to be the last
         touch
In a sweat and with a tear...I awake
Reach for a cigarette and start to shake
"If that's what it takes for me to get her..."
I reach for the gun and pull the trigger

Black rose
11/03/2003

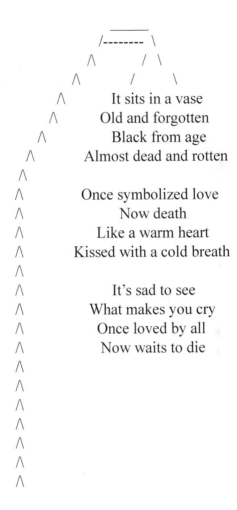

It sits in a vase
Old and forgotten
Black from age
Almost dead and rotten

Once symbolized love
Now death
Like a warm heart
Kissed with a cold breath

It's sad to see
What makes you cry
Once loved by all
Now waits to die

Joker
12/04/2003

You hear them laugh
You hear them cry
They follow you
You don't know why

With sharp white teeth
And dark black eyes
They are undead
From the graves they rise

Scared to death
They leave you be
"Can't sleep
Clowns will eat me."

Dead Man Walking
01/13/2004

Blessed are the dead
        The rain falls near
                For their screams are like
                        A whisper in my ear

Blessed are the dead
        That rot in the ground
                Rising from their graves
                        Like a Merry-go-round

Blessed are the dead
        Who haunt my dreams
                Watching the night sky
                        I can hear their screams

Blessed are the dead
        Who follow me near
                For I am the reaper
                        The living do fear

Living Hell
06/28/2005

An angel with clipped wings, such a sad sight to see
    Struggling to get by, how could this be?
An angel with clipped wings, and no place to go
    You can stay with me angel, and I will love
    you so

An angel with clipped wings, Why do you cry?
    With so much to live for, yet waiting to die
An angel with clipped wings, so far away from home
    Dropped off in the middle of no where, and
    left to roam

An angel with clipped wings, I know not what to do
    I try and try and try, but you won't let me
    help you
An angel with clipped wings, and wounds not yet
healed
    The key to your heart, and the vault that is
    sealed

An angel with clipped wings, you can not go
    You will not survive, and I need you so
An angel with clipped wings, left behind to die
    I'll remember you angel, and the day the
    angel cried!

I shed a tear
11/11/2006

I shed a tear yesterday and as I saw it hit the ground
        I watched the next one form and heard the dripping
        sound
I shed a tear yesterday and I'm not quite sure why
        More and more came, but I did not cry
I shed a tear yesterday but didn't ask to talk
        I didn't need no one's help, I didn't go for a walk
I shed a tear yesterday and right after it was over
        Right after it dried and right before I became
        sober

I shed some blood yesterday as the knife dripped its tear
        A moment of euphoria...it all became clear
I shed a tear yesterday and before you ask why
        Let me tell you this, I didn't want to die

I don't know why the tear had come
Or why it shined so red
But it wasn't a tear of water
But of blood instead
I'm feeling very calm now
As the pain does fade behind
And I can see the truth
Though my eyes are blind
I shed a tear yesterday
And today I will too
I'm sorry if it hurts
But now you know what I go through

Reflect
3/10/2011

The dark place I go
The black I see
The demons in my world
That follow me
I feel the clutch
Of the Devil's own grasp
Around my heart
Beat it fast
And in the empty
And baron streets
I am alone
With the maker I meet
Face to face
With the demon of hell
The ultimate Angel
From heaven he fell
My soul is his
Already dead and black
I don't have the want
To try to take it back
This demon is death

And he haunts my every thought
His image in my mirror
The pain he brought
The devil I imagine
In the image I see
A devil from hell
My devil is me

Warning
3/11/2011

The devil dreams
Of angel Hymnns
Where thunder fades
And lighting dims
What dreams may come
What hell bound flesh
Damned to flame
The sinners rest
And glow does fire
By bone it burns
True is torture
And all will learn
Beware the pain
That may await
For those who fail
To keep the faith
A deal on earth
No soul does spare
Nor Hail Mary from
The Devil's care
So choose your course
Beware your fate
For those who sin
The devil wait

My own Heaven
3/12/2011

If I wind up surrounded by clouds
I'm going to ask to leave
Because heaven for me
Is my grandma's house on Christmas Eve
There's a dog named pug
Guarding the door
And all us grandkids
Playing on the floor
There's pizza and soda
And presents too
Always a warm hug
As a greeting to you
But more importantly there's family
All with smiles on their face
Because there's no sadness here
It's not allowed in this place

I think about them often
And miss them a lot
With a tear in my eye
And hearts empty spot
But I know I'll see them
Guarded by a light
On a future Christmas Eve
If heaven gets it right
But whether on earth or in heaven
We don't ever say good-byes
Because no matter what happens
Love never dies

LIFE

*"The punch line's life, but
I don't get the joke."*

The Sun Will Rise
3/03/2003

Today I see fire
Burning inside
I said I was okay
But I lied
> *Today I want to die*
> *My heart is torn*
> *Every moment I wish*
> *I was never born*
>> *Today is filled with sadness*
>> *Depression in the air*
>> *As I think of my last kiss*
>> *And how she didn't care*

But tomorrow is a new day and the sun will rise
And tomorrow I will forgive, yesterday's lies...

Warrior
3/27/2003

He stands tall, and will not break for no man
He is unmoved on the course he will make
Pursuing what he wants, because he can
And whatever he wants, he will just take

Lean on him, and know you will not fall ever
He's a god with power to fight
He will never stop, he does not know never
He is a god from early day to night

A warrior is a man who is strong
He builds walls to block out the pain once felt
He knows what is right, and can do no wrong
The walls he builds of ice and can not melt

He's on his toes, and is always alert
If he lets no one close he won't be hurt

Rain Drops
4/29/2003

They
fall like
the sun
at night.
The sadness
They bring, makes
A light heart heavy
And can even kill a king.
Some keep them in, while
Others let them drip. They roll down
Your face, until they find your lip.
Though rain drops fall, but I don't
talk of that hear. So much pain
brought from a single
tear.

Good Times
5/12/2003

To focus on the tough, can make you sad
To focus on the anger, can make you mad
Bleeding wounds heal, and hearts can grow
Happiness blocked away, can sometimes show

To ignore the good, is to live in the dark
Don't speed through life, but don't sit in park
Life is tough, and sometimes it will rain
But that's life; try not to live in the pain

Rain can be fun, with someone by your side
Like a lighthouse to a ship, they help to guide
So to those who wish to die
Lift your head, please don't cry

The sun will shine, in the days to come
So smile at life, and have some fun

Writing
8/18/2003

The words aren't coming as easy
anymore
I don't know what to say
I'm losing my mind I know it
I can feel it floating away
Every day I grow crazier
It's starting to scare me
My minds starting to leave
If only you could see
What good is a writer
Who can't write
Question its worth
Is it worth the fight
I'm starting to go insane
It's the beginning of the end
I just hope one day
I can find my life again

Power – It's Effects
11/07/2003

Personal

Obstacles

Weakening

Emotional

Resolve

Thank you
7/13/2004

Not born with the same blood
Or in the same family tree
But with out asking questions
You took care of me
Taught me right from wrong
I didn't always hear
But you gave me a shoulder to cry on
And a cloth to wipe my tear
You gave me memories I love
And even a place to stay
You made time to listen
Even when I had nothing to say
I have brothers and sisters
Cousins and friends
Your patience wears thin
But your love never ends
I never said I was smart
Or even clever
But I know its unconditional love
Because family' forever
You gave me confidence
To be what I want to be
But my love and thanks to you
Is because you gave me a family

Content
7/15/2004

I don't know when it happened
But something filled the hole
And I've come to realize
I've found content in my soul
The anger has diminished
And the depression seemed to fade
For once in my life
I'm glad that I stayed
I have found light
At the end of the tunnel
Who knows what's to come
All I can do is wonder
The possibilities are endless
As I start to see
I can happily say good-bye
To yesterday's me

When I think of you
7/31/2006

I think there is a bond
A connection with me and you
I think there's nothing for each other
That we wouldn't do
I think there's no topic left silent
No joke left untold
I think there's no letter left unwritten
With special words left unbold
I think there's never a moment
You're not on my mind
I think there's no words I could say
That wouldn't be kind
I think there's a friendship
That is larger than us
I think there's no way to break
This strong bound of trust
I think of this
And one thing remains true
I think of this
Only when I think of you

Good Things Come
2/20/2007

This I write
To those who wish
To those who love
The ones they miss
To those who pray
To those who sigh
To those who hope
And those who try
To those who want
To those who need
To those who plant
Loves little seed
This I write
To those who cry
To those who push
With no reply

To those who look
To those who smile
To those who think
This may take awhile
To those who dream
And believe in fate
Cause good things come
To those who wait

Him
4/15/2005

He lives in the depth of our minds,
where your soul starts to weep
He crawls around in your heart,
to the point you can't sleep
With the power of a king, but
the vengeance of the poor
He grows and grows and grows
until you can't take it anymore
He eats at you inside-out, to
the point you start to scream
You try to wake yourself up,
but it is not a dream
He attacks just you... and
won't stop till your dead
He crawls up your soul
and into your head
The brain is his labyrinth,
each turn makes you crazy
Your body starts to shake...
your vision gets hazy
Some on the outside know

Others turn away
And those that stop and stare
Don't know what to say
You should live in fear
This could happen to you
It's scary to think
What depression can do

Soul
2/10/2006

I am your body, your mind
Your spirit, your essence
I am the core of your world
I am the heart of your character
I am your psyche

I die at times
Bits of me being sold for the greater good
Life's justice for an eternity of torture
I'm the indefinable yet inescapable
I'm your prison, your freedom
I'm your grip on reality
That drives you insane

I am you…but not
I am before you
I am after you
I am in you
And around you
I am everything, and nothing
I am your body's god
        Worship me
I can destroy you
        I am…
        I can…

Dream
2/10/2006

I am the minds perception of life
    The awakened thoughts of the
    unawakened
I am your horror, your love
    Your minds clutch on the broken
    leg of reality
    Your justice, your lost life
    Your truth in a world of lies
When you weep over her
I show you her face
When you get depressed
I show you a life better than yours
I am your torture, your pain, your death
    ...slow painful death
But you long for me
You look forward to my visits
Like an addiction
    I am your crack
I bring you pleasure and pain in visions
My truth is your guilt
However the most inescapable fact:

I am you
You and your torture
You are your pain
You are your slow death
You are what you long for
The true you

This is Why
8/4/2005

"Why'd you join?" asked a friend
"You do realize this could mean your end
And that bullet holes do mend
But they can also make you dead"
And all I said was…."because"
"Shit they aint do shit to me
And my life aint free
So I'll stay right here please"
"But it's the right thing to do"
"Shit maybe for you
but I'm sorry I got to be true
Fuck, what they gonna do….to me?
I'm trying to make you see
They aint do shit to me
So right here is where I need to be"

While they kill your fellow man
And females get the back of a hand
Just because a man is mad
Seven year old kids weighing 15 lbs
And war planes go round and round
Where they kill woman and children
And we fight a war we can't win
Just for a pat on the back and a purple pin
Little food and hot weather
Promises of how life will get better
Sleeping with bugs, and a gun
Dreaming how this use to be fun
Men give their lives, husbands lose wives

Parents lose kids, and kids lose parents
Here or there is doesn't matter where it it
…I risk my life so you CAN stay here
While MY mother sheds her tears
Only 18 years old and killing a man
At 24 having flash backs of the sand
So you can talk your shit about what you wouldn't do
And how this shit aint for you
And how I'm the fool
But please one rule…
Start with two words…"Thank you"
And give me the respect we both know is due!

Friend?
11/12/2006

You can talk all the bullshit you want
                    But my life aint for you, it's for me
Happy with your blue skies?
                    Well with gray ones it's hard to see
Life can get you under
                    Make you feel you should quit
          And all the help you try to give…
Well with my life it doesn't fit
                    That's right, roll your eyes
          It's just me speaking stupid again
Always trying to get attention
                    Spoken like a true friend
"He'll be ok…"
                                        "He'll pull through…"
Yeah well what if I don't want to?
                              Words are my release
Poetry is how I feel
                    So what do you think I wonder
When you ignore what is real
          I'm not going to try killing myself
                    Not again…so don't worry
Just keep standing there
                    Like my judge and my jury
Is it so hard to pick up the phone
          Take five seconds to say, "hi
          I was thinking about you
I love you and good-bye."
                    Is that to much to ask?
                    For you to show you care

"It's not right to ask that"
                        Yea well life aint fair
I'm sorry if I'm just a burden
                Just too much for you to handle
But when I die
                    Don't light a fucking candle
Just keep thinking I was too much
                And don't you dare cry for me then
Don't weep over my grave
                        That's what I ask of you
…friend

If I could Do it All Again
1/27/2007

If I could do it all again
      I would pay attention in school
If I could do it all again
      I wouldn't act so much like a fool
If I could do it all again
      I wouldn't have so many scars
If I could do it all again
      I would have wished upon more stars
If I could do it all again
      I wouldn't have had drugs in my life
If I could do it all again
      I wouldn't have been so quick to grab the
knife
If I could do it all again
      I wouldn't treat life like a game
But if I could do it all again
      I would keep you and I the same

Prison
1/27/2007

I am not just behind bars
Or kept in a cell
I am not just the keeper of a key
To the locked gates of hell
      I'm the loneliness of far-away
      The depression of alone
      The tears in the eyes
      Of a good-bye on the phone
            I'm the trapped heart of forever
            With the uncertainty of tomorrow
            The happiness of together
            That brings so much sorrow
      I'm the inability to leave
      Mixed with the desire to go
      The wishful thinking of "us"
      That you're not sure you know

A prison can be open
As long as you're not free to leave
This open place I'm in
Is my prison to me

Take it or leave it
2/12/2007

It's 5% imagination
And about 12% trust
It's around 18% anger
And at least 20% lust
It's 28% putting up with shit
And 34% fighting to change
It's 40% moving fast through life
And 47% pulling the reigns
It's 50% respect for others
But 55% respect for yourself
It's 60% independence
And 61% asking for help
It's 65% hate
And 69% love
It's 75% waiting for "it"
And 80% giving "it" a shove
It's 89% bad times
And 90% good
It's 92% doing what you want
And 98% wishing you could
Everyone's percent is different
So feel free to rewrite
But keep one thing the same
It's 100% life

A Good Father
2/12/2007

I have the things I need to live
And the power to atone
Given to me by your hands
Whose fingers were worked to the bone

I have the pictures of my youth
In the frames that I do smash
Taken by the man I love
Who stayed behind the flash

I have the words of kindness
That helped my through and through
Spoken by the lips of him
Whose heart was truly blue

I have an image of a man
That I wish I could be
A memory of the one
Who gave so much for me

I know that you are tired now
And your heart is awfully sad
But I thank you for teaching me
What it takes to be a dad